C000109648

household management for men

First published in Great Britain in 2004 by
Cassell Illustrated
2-4 Heron Quays
London
E14 4JP

A CIP catalogue record for this book is
available from the British Library.

ISBN 1-84403272-8
9781844032723

Conceived, designed and produced by
Quid Publishing
Fourth Floor
Sheridan House
112-116A Western Road
Hove BN3 1DD
England
www.quidpublishing.com

Publisher: Nigel Browning
Publishing Manager: Sophie Martin
Author: Jane Moseley
Project Management: Essential Works
Illustrations: Matt Pagett

Printed and bound in China by
Midas Printing International Ltd

NOTE
Every effort has been taken to ensure that
all information in this book is correct and
compatible with national standards at the
time of publication. This book is not
intended to replace manufacturers'
instructions in the use of their tools or
products – always follow their safety
guidelines.

The author, publisher and copyright holder
assume no responsibility for any injury,
loss or damage caused or sustained as a
consequence of the use and application of
the contents of this book.

A LITTLE BOOK OF DOMESTIC WISDOM

kitchen

household management for men

Contents

The Art and Science of Domestic Wisdom   8

How To Use This Book   10

Know Your Kitchen   12

Learn, Earn and Burn   14

Questionnaire   16

Weekly Wonders, Monthly Miracles, Annual Asks   18

Domestic God: Top-to-Toe   20

A Day in the Life of a Kitchen God   22

Don't be a Kitchen Klutz   24

Kitchen Clever   26

Kitchen Confidential   28

Tools: Knives   30

Tools: Pans   32

Tools: Glasses   34

The History of the Refrigerator   36

Keeping it Cool   38

Keeping Things on Ice   40

👤	Good Refrigerator/Bad Refrigerator	42
🍳	What's in Store	44
👤	Food Facts	46
🍳	Carving a Whole Chicken	48
🍳	Making a Cocktail	50
🍳	Whose Turn to Wash the Dishes?	52
🍳	Taking the Heat in the Kitchen	54
🧹	Washing Floors and Windows	56
🧹	Washing and Wiping	58
🧹	Stain Removal	60
👤	Plant an Idea	62
👤	Petiquette	64
🧹	Bug Off	66
👤	Shortcuts	68
✋	Do it Together	70
👤	Wise Dude Mess Mantra	72
👤	QED → QAD	74
👤	A Miscellany of Domestic Wisdom	76

Kitchen

'A good kitchen should be sufficiently remote from the principal apartments of the house, that the members, visitors, or guests of the family, may not perceive the odour incident to cooking, or hear the noise of culinary operations.'

MRS ISABELLA BEETON, BOOK OF HOUSEHOLD MANAGEMENT, 1861

| Technique | Tool | Wisdom | Cleaning | Chore |

The Art and Science of Domestic Wisdom

Let's start with a few little-known but interesting facts. Household management is both a science and an art; it uses both sides of the male brain and is a practical and spiritual exercise – practical because it establishes order, hygiene and safety within the home environment; spiritual because it makes you feel more comfortable and secure within your own four walls (plus rather pleased with yourself). Even better, housework is also an aerobic exercise that allows you to flex your muscles and push your weight about at home without annoying people.

Housework is not dull, boring or a waste of leisure hours that could be better spent in front of a television or at the bar. It saves time, creates order out of chaos, burns calories and makes you sexier. Are you more interested now? Read on.

Men, when questioned about how much housework they do, often reply: 'Not my department,' 'Far too busy at work,' 'What's the point? It always looks the same five minutes later,' and 'Do you reckon Hercules did the dusting?' However, in our fast-changing world, increasing numbers of men share the household chores or, indeed, assume full responsibility for them. The dynamics are changing. Real men do housework – it's a fact. And real men get rewards.

The Little Book of Domestic Wisdom demonstrates how to approach household tasks positively and effectively, how to schedule, organize and execute tasks

efficiently – just like any other job that lands in the daily in-tray – and shows how to enjoy a similar sense of achievement and fulfillment. Some jobs are more rewarding than others: dusting, like filing, can pile up and stare you in the face for some time without any major repercussions, but neglecting the kitchen sink or the laundry basket will lead to instant inconvenience. However, just think how great you feel when the filing tray is empty. It's the same with housework. And you haven't got the journey home afterwards.

What to do when

Don't let the very thought of housework overwhelm you, just like a huge work project upon which you cannot get started. Ease yourself into it and do a little each day. Don't wait until things get completely out of control before tackling them – tasks will take twice the amount of time and be half as effective. To do it properly you need a system, a routine and a schedule. 'Diarize, prioritize, realize' is a good mission statement – it works just as well at home as on the time management course and in the office.

First things first

Individuals should assume responsibility for their own clutter. Taking ownership of a problem is half way to solving it. Admitting to ownership of a pair of odorous socks under the sofa is the first step on the road to removing, washing, folding and finding them a good home. Don't upset people by de-junking their possessions without consultation. It would be like reading their post and dumping it without their knowledge or consent. Set a time schedule for the 'house de-junk' and stick to it.

If some tasks are going to take more than a few days (eg clearing an attic groaning with possessions, unopened packing cases, lots of trash, some treasure and mountains of dust) you will need to come up with a few long-term goals rather than immediate ones.

A little every day goes a long way

You will feel so much better when you get up in the morning if you have cleared up after your evening meal, taken the dirty dishes into the kitchen, washed and stored them, tidied the living area and sorted out your laundry and clothes for the next day. Equally, on returning from a hard day's work at the office or in the library, the feel-good factor for you and your housemates or partner goes up dramatically if the place looks tidy and clean. It is welcoming and nurturing – it makes you feel better. Even cavemen felt better when the cave looked more like a home than a butcher's shop.

Mess attracts mess – it's a fact. Three lonely and unwashed plates by the sink are quickly joined by three potential mates – they reproduce easily and soon you have a little family. If someone else can leave dishes unwashed, why can't you? Hold on a minute, though – what if someone pops round unannounced – your boss, friend or potential romantic interest perhaps? How impressed would they be to find the house in a total mess? Romance can be hard to kindle and sustain amid empty beer cans and the unappealing, pungent remains of last night's takeout. The smell of stale food is a highly effective passion killer. Underwear that has hitchhiked into the living area in less than pristine condition doesn't even bear thinking about.

How To Use This Book

This book is aimed at a fairly wide audience – male students, young and not-so-young working men, whether single, married or in partnerships, stay-at-home men, both novices and experienced home managers, together with all the women out there who want to pass on the art of household management to their menfolk, whatever their age or previous knowledge. Some readers will be new to household management, others may have a little or even a lot of experience. They can derive some satisfaction from already having a few techniques and tips under their belt. Beginners will soon get the hang of things and move speedily from the nursery slopes to intermediate status. By page 80, all of you will be experts in the art and science of household management and ready to tackle a few off-piste tasks.

The key to understanding the principles of household management is to read, digest and implement the advice in the *Little Book of Domestic Wisdom*. Pass on what you learn, what you achieve, even what you do wrong. People like to hear about successes and failures on the domestic front and thereby imitate or deviate.

Since time began, wisdom has been passed down orally from generation to generation. Cavemen and women sat round the fire and taught their young how to keep the hearth warm, how to barbecue the wildlife and make duvet covers from their fur. Wisdom learnt at one's parents' knee led to the Barbecue Age becoming the Iron Age and then the Modern Age (with a few eras in between). Continue the tradition. Do it subtly, though. Don't drag

Domestic God

 Look out for the Domestic God icon if you want to fast-track to the heart of the matter (or that of your partner).

your partner or housemate around the 21st-century cave by their metaphorical loincloths, telling them what to do in a smug, been-there-done-that-ironed-the-dinosaur-T-shirt kind of way. Share your knowledge gently. Share the housework, too (see page 70). Don't fight over it – buy them a copy for their birthday.

Rewarding times

We all need to feel congratulated or pampered from time to time, particularly when we have faced a challenge and successfully tackled it. Make sure you reward yourself (if nobody else is going to do it for you) by patting yourself metaphorically on the back and treating yourself to something that makes you feel good – a new book, CD or DVD, a massage, or a bottle of good wine. Tell someone what you've done. You are feeling better already.

Dirty Devil

 Keep an eye out for the Dirty Devil as a warning not to go there, do this, think that, or even suggest the other.

Know Your ...

Kitchen

The message in the kitchen is SSS not SOS. Spick, Span and Spotless is the order of the day. Not Save Our Soul or Sort Out Salmonella or even Smelly Old Scoff. Keeping things in tip-top condition in the HQ is the number one task of the Numero Uno Household Management Agent. 007 days a week.

1 WINDOWS
Wash your windows regularly to improve the atmosphere and the light.

2 PLANT LIFE
Herbs generally thrive on a sunny windowsill.

3 KEEP IT CLEAN
Sink and worktop hygiene is extremely important in the kitchen. Keep everyday equipment on the worktop and store the rest.

4 THE OVEN
Wipe tiles and walls near the oven every day. Clean your oven more than once in a blue moon.

5 CLOTH CLEANING
Clean your cloths and tea towels every couple of days.

6 FRIDGE
Keep the door firmly closed. Literally and metaphorically. It is not a storage alternative for food that is out of date and out of fashion.

Learn, Earn and Burn

Life is all about learning. Domestic life has its very own learning curves, some more vertical than others. To scale and conquer, you need to focus. The art of household management can be divided into three key areas: Learn, Earn and Burn.

Three Small Steps for Mankind

1 LEARN

Learn the principles of housework – not just the 'what' but the 'why', 'how', 'when' and 'where' involved. It is the first big, important step along the highway to hygiene heaven. The *Little Book of Domestic Wisdom* will explain all these aspects. It will reveal the dangers of not cleaning your home, the secret hazards involved and the risks you are running. It will unravel the mystery of an ancient art made simpler by modern technology. Look what happened when Aladdin tried a spot of polishing on the brass lamp. The same new world could open up to you with just a little effort.

2 EARN

Earn the brownie points and reap the benefits, physical, spiritual and emotional, of mastering what are essentially simple but rewarding (in many senses) techniques. Housework is good for you. It helps keep you hygienic and therefore appealing, it brings with it gold stars and brownie points, and it helps put a new, improved shine on that domestic halo you have been hiding under your dusty bushel all this time. Your romantic, emotional health will get a spring clean.

3 BURN

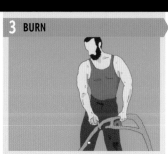

And, lastly, burn those calories as you master this important art. It is cheaper than going to the gym, it doesn't involve a commute and you kill two birds plus a zillion potential allergens and unpleasant germs with one proverbial stone, swoop of the cloth or flourish of the vacuum. Exercise reduces stress, helps trigger the happy hormones and builds muscle. Housework is indoor exercise. You can choose your own time and your own background music. You are never far from a reviving drink or nourishing snack. What more could you want?

THE WHOLE EQUATION

Let's look at the whole equation:

Where
DW+S = **D**omestic **W**isdom plus **S**atisfaction

and
hm = household management
w = weekly
d = daily
cb = calories burned
mb = muscle built

$$DW+S = hm \ (w) + 250cb + mb + 1.9\%$$

$$DW+S^2 = hm \ (d) + 500cb + mb + 3.5\%$$

👼 Add to this Equation ...

Add to this equation the Domestic God factor and it suddenly starts to add up and make sense. The statistics are even more attractive when you add your potential brownie points (bp) and personal appeal (pa). It is a win-win situation.

Questionnaire

It is time to ask yourself some serious (and some not quite so serious) questions. Have a go at this quick questionnaire to find out just how much you do know about the subject of household management. If you get more questions

Do You Know it all Already?

How long should you generally leave an opened jar of food in the refrigerator?
A) A COUPLE OF DAYS
B) A COUPLE OF WEEKS
C) A COUPLE OF MONTHS
D) UNTIL IT WALKS OUT ON YOU
E) UNTIL YOUR PARTNER FINDS IT

Why should you remove dust regularly from surfaces?
A) IT GETS UP YOUR PARTNER'S NOSE
B) THERE IS NEVER ENOUGH TO WRITE YOUR WHOLE NAME IN
C) IT IS FULL OF DEAD DUST MITES AND CAN CAUSE ALLERGIES
D) IT SPOILS THE VIEW ON THE TELEVISION SCREEN
E) YOU DON'T NEED TO – JUST TURN THE LIGHTS DOWN

When did you last empty the trash?
A) LAST NIGHT
B) LAST WEEK
C) LAST MONTH
D) DON'T KNOW WHERE IT IS
E) NEVER

Is your dog more hygienic than you?
A) YES
B) NO
C) IT'S A CLOSE SHAVE
D) ABOUT THE SAME
E) I DON'T HAVE A DOG

When should you do the washing up?
A) AS SOON AS POSSIBLE AFTER A MEAL
B) ONCE A WEEK
C) ONCE A MONTH
D) JUST BEFORE YOUR MOTHER ARRIVES
E) WHEN YOU RUN OUT OF PLATES

right than wrong, you are weaving your way to wisdom but by no means are you an all-knowing, all-powerful household cleaning agent. If you get more wrong than right, you need this book badly.

Why should you ventilate your kitchen regularly?
A) TO TEMPT THE NEIGHBOURS WITH THE SMELL OF YOUR COOKING
B) TO GET RID OF THE SMELL OF YOUR COOKING
C) TO REMOVE THE ODOURS FROM THE FRIDGE WHEN YOU OPEN IT
D) SO THAT YOU CAN THROW YOUR CIGARETTE OUT
E) TO CONTROL MOISTURE PRODUCED BY COOKING

Why do you need to install a smoke detector?
A) TO CHECK YOUR PARTNER HAS NOT TAKEN UP SMOKING AGAIN
B) TO ALERT YOU TO SMOKE AND PREVENT FIRES
C) I DON'T SMOKE, I DON'T NEED ONE
D) TO LET YOU KNOW THE FOOD IS READY
E) HAVEN'T GOT THE FOGGIEST

When did you last clean your refrigerator?
A) LAST MONTH
B) LAST YEAR
C) LAST LEAP YEAR
D) I CLEAN IT EVERY MONTH
E) I THOUGHT IT WAS SELF-CLEANING

Scientists have found that the male brain doesn't register dust. Is this because:
A) THE SCIENTISTS WERE ALL MALE
B) DUST DOES NOT EXIST
C) DUST DOES NOT MATTER
D) MATTER DOES NOT EXIST
E) DUST MATTER IS TOO COMPLEX

What is your mess motto?
A) A TIDY KITCHEN IS A SAFE KITCHEN
B) MESS IS CREATIVE AND I CREATE MESS
C) MESS DOESN'T MATTER
D) MY MESS IS YOUR MESS
E) MY LITTLE MESS DOESN'T MATTER WHEN THE WORLD IS IN A BIGGER ONE

Weekly Wonders, Monthly Miracles, Annual Asks

Establishing a routine for chores is important. It's just the same as at the office – a macro and micro analysis. It helps you see the bigger picture. Consider all the jobs that have to be done and create a list or chart that

Chore Chart:

ANNUALLY:
- PULL OUT REFRIGERATOR AND OVEN TO CLEAN BEHIND AND UNDER THEM
- WASH BLINDS
- CLEAN CEILINGS AND WALLS

MONTHLY:
- CLEAN OVEN (OK, QUARTERLY)
- WASH WINDOWS
- DUST BLINDS AND SHADES
- WASH MIRRORS
- GIVE FANS A QUICK DUST (CEILING AND FREESTANDING ONES, NOT YOUR ADMIRERS)
- CHECK SUPPLIES IN LARDER AND FREEZER

divides them into four headings: annually, monthly (or quarterly), weekly (or fortnightly if you are very lazy) and daily. Hourly is taking the whole micro stuff just too far... sticking to a weekly schedule really does work.

WEEKLY:

- CLEAR AND CLEAN REFRIGERATOR
- WIPE DOWN OVEN AND OTHER APPLIANCES (IN AND OUT)
- CLEAN SINKS
- SCRUB FLOORS
- DO INVENTORY OF REFRIGERATOR AND PANTRY FOR FRESH STAPLE SUPPLIES
- WASH OUT AND SANITIZE TRASH BIN
- REPLACE KITCHEN CLOTHS WITH CLEAN ONES (TWO TO THREE TIMES A WEEK)
- SORT OUT RECYCLING SUPPLIES

DAILY:

- CLEAR CLUTTER
- TIDY AND CLEAN SURFACES
- WASH DIRTY DISHES
- SWEEP AND CLEAN FLOOR
- PUT OUT CLEAN KITCHEN CLOTHS IF NECESSARY
- WIPE TRASH BIN AND EMPTY IF NECESSARY
- DO INTERIM SHOPPING
- WATER PLANTS AND CHECK FLOWERS

Domestic God: Top-to-Toe

There is no point making a valiant attempt to keep your home in order if you fail to pay similar attention to your body. Is it not a temple after all? Look after your physique in the kitchen. The GSOH rule applies to you, too (see page 24).

Top-to-Toe Hygiene Routine

Eyes

You won't get 20/20 vision if you're myopic (aka shortsighted), but eating bilberries could well improve your eyesight. Full of antioxidants, too, they are like carrots on the efficient ocular maintenance front. Eye Eye, kitchen captain. And which vegetable makes a grown man cry? The onion, of course. Pop it in the freezer for ten minutes or the refrigerator for an hour to stop the tears.

Nose

Keep it clean and clear so you can detect leaks, the presence of mould and food that has gone off. Help it out by ventilating your kitchen and improving the circulation of fresh air. Garlic has anti-viral properties and helps your immune system and fights off colds and flu, so cook with it or take capsules. Date a Mediterranean and kissing won't be an issue. Don't smoke.

Mouth

Inextricably linked to the stomach, this is the port of entry for your body. Eat better, feel better. You are what you eat. Start a food diary or a drink diary or, hey, what about a joint one (definitely not that sort, silly...). Then you can see every little thing you eat and drink, even those 'harmless' snacks and that 'just a quick beer' after work. Cut the fat off meat before cooking, go for low-fat milk in sauces, go for grilled rather than battered fish. Try to have two alcohol-free days a week. Cut out spirits. Have a wine-free January. Try low-cal drinks. Buy interesting alcohol-free drinks instead.

Hands and Arms

Always wash your hands thoroughly before and after preparing food. Hands and wrists, too. Count to ten. Dry hands on a paper towel or specific hand towel, not the tea towel, dishcloth or your partner.

Use proper oven mitts to protect yourself from burns when cooking. Keep a supply of sturdy gloves near your cooking area. Don't toss wet foods into frying pans with lots of oil – you may be splattered with hot oil. If you do incur a minor burn, cool the area under running water for 15 minutes to lower the skin temperature, numb the pain and reduce swelling. Applying butter or grease is a no-no.

Body

Wear an apron to protect clothing and your body parts. Don't cook in the nude. It is healthy to eat naked food (washed, raw carrots, fruit and salad, for example) but not food, naked (it's a grammar thing). Get fresh, though. That's fine, although tinned or frozen fruit and veg is OK but watch out for extra salt or sugar by reading the labels. In general, go easy on salt and sugar. If you feel like spicing things up, turmeric (the spice found in curries) has anti-inflammatory properties and chilli peppers are thought to have fat-burning ones. They work off additional calories by triggering a thermodynamic burn that can last up to five hours after eating, thereby speeding up the metabolism and preventing new fat forming. Put peppers into small meals throughout the day rather than a huge one at night or lunch. Say goodbye to butter on your baked potato and add salsa. Spark up your salad with hot peppers or add to your stir-fry. Burn, baby, burn. Exercise in the kitchen. Burn calories with vigorous surface, floor and wall cleaning.

Technique Tool Wisdom Cleaning Chore

A Day in the Life of a Kitchen God

As established, the kitchen is the HQ of the household operation. At weekends you will be in and out of it all day (and possibly all evening and night, if you are entertaining or a Midnight Muncher). On weekdays, visits to the hub may be

Domestic God's Kitchen Routine

6–7:00am

MORNING, KITCHEN. MORNING, PARDNA. Let's assume (optimistically?) that the kitchen doesn't greet you with the unpleasant and stale reminders of the night before. Your partner will (hopefully) greet you with a smile and a cuppa.

7:10am

KICKSTART THE DAY It may be steaming, freshly-brewed coffee. But hold on a minute, guys. By starting the day with a cup of hot water and a slice of lemon or a cup of green tea, you can cleanse the system first thing. Coffeeholics will find this bit hard.

7:30am

WHIZZ TO WORK If you have time before work, or if it is the weekend, whizz up a fresh fruit mix or add semi-skimmed milk and low-fat yogurt to make a smoothie. Add fresh ginger or ginseng for the extra zing. Increase its anti-oxidant powers by adding blueberries.

11:00am

SNACK ATTACK Try winning the Snack Wars with an apple or banana, walnuts, a rice cake or a glass of water. Count your coffees. Remember caffeine makes you tired and irritable. Stick to just a couple in the morning. Water keeps the engine cool, literally.

12:30–2:00pm

GRAB AND GO Think about what you eat at lunchtime. A light meal keeps the engine ticking over nicely. Sandwiches are popular with guys on the go and are not a bad idea. Get your protein from the filling – cold meat, fish, eggs, cheese, beans, tofu.

4:00pm

MID-ARVO MUNCHIES Uh-oh. Time to get fruity again. How about a few strawberries? Share them with colleagues. A stick of raw broccoli is full of nutrients but better for your body than your image. Eat it in the stationery cupboard (alone, probably).

restricted to pre- and post-work for brekky, home-alone snacks, supper with your partner or dinner with chums. The following regime is a one-size-fits-all guide. Adapt it. It covers eating at the office – deskfast and lunch.

7:45am

I AM TOO BUSY FOR BREAKFAST Running on empty doesn't work for your car, so why should it work for you? Start the engine, warm it up first thing and you're ready to roll for the day. Cereal, toast, juice – none of it takes very long to prepare.

8:00am

DESKFAST Boil an egg the night before and munch it en route or at your desk with a handful of dried fruit. Dried organic apricots and a low-fat bio yogurt will help get the brain in third gear. Mixed nuts and you're cruising.

9:30am

BIG SUNDAY BREAKFAST OK, spoil yourself at the weekend, but not literally. Try grilling instead of frying your bacon, sausage and mushroom, and poach the egg. Toast the bread instead of frying. Freshly squeeze oranges, no sugar in your beverage.

6:00pm

HOLD THE CRISPS Off to the bar or the fridge after work for the evening's first beer or glass of wine? Limit the number of crisps or roasted nuts you eat. Save your calorie intake for later. How many people have put their not-so-clean fingers in that bowl of mixed nuts?

7–8:00pm

TAKE-OUT OR TIME-OUT? You are tired. Take some time-out to debrief after work and then head for the kitchen. Try to prepare your own meal a few times a week. It is social, it will spoil your partner and not your appetite (or your budget).

12:00 midnight

MIDNIGHT MUNCHIES Off to the refrigerator in your sexy slippers with a torch? Don't spoil things by eating double cream out of the pot. How about a handful of strawberries with low-fat yogurt, goat's cheese on a rice cracker or raw carrot with hummus?

| Technique | Tool | Wisdom | Cleaning | Chore |

Don't be a Kitchen Klutz

'House-proud Wise Guy WLTM similar with GSOH for long-term domestic bliss.' No, it does not stand for 'good sense of humour.' GSOH means Great Safety, Order and Hygiene. These attributes are key to a kitchen and a successful

Domestic God's No-Nos

1. All Washed Up

In the context of the kitchen, 'all washed up' is a very positive condition and one to which you should aspire. Unwashed dishes are not only visually unappealing, but also provide a perfect home for organisms invisible to the naked eye. In those countries where cockroaches and other ugly, resourceful insects are regular, if unwanted, houseguests, these are rather more macro than micro. Piles of dirty dishes and pans are nasty on all fronts, and, what's more, you risk running out of clean crockery and glasses.

2. Trash the Trash

Overflowing, unwashed trash bins are also high on the no-no list for many of the same reasons. They are unattractive, unsavoury, unhygienic – the list of 'uns' goes on and on. Take the trash out every evening and give the bin a quick wipe before putting a new bin liner inside. Once a week wash it out thoroughly. Keep a lid on your trash – you know it makes sense.

Dirty Devil says ...

Avoid kitchen hell by becoming the
patron saint of sterlising.

domestic partnership. To achieve and then maintain them is your mission. As
with most missions, rules apply. There are things you must and must not do.
Here are some of the Klutz traps to avoid.

3. Wipe, Wash, Dry

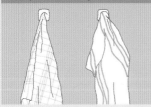

What's the big deal? A cloth is a cloth
is a cloth, isn't it? Wrong. Cloths have
vocations. Dishcloths should be devoted
to washing dishes and worktops; tea towels
are dedicated to drying the dishes and
floor cloths should only ever be used for
mopping up spills and things on the floor.
Towels were invented to dry your hands.
You must be similarly single-minded in
your role as kitchen carer – failing to
wash cloths regularly is negligence of the
highest domestic order. Dirty cloths are
hazardous to your health and have to go.

4. Surface Tension

After preparing a meal, wipe down all
working surfaces, removing food, grease
and other debris. Dirty worktops, ovens
and sinks are health and safety hazards.
What's more, they are unlikely to be
the first thing you relish seeing in the
morning, particularly if you are feeling
rather delicate. The cat might enjoy that
pool of sticky, smelly tuna oil in the sink,
but you will not find its residual odour
as tempting when it greets you the next
day. It takes seconds to wipe down all
the surfaces – it takes hours to remove
the consequences of inaction.

Kitchen Clever

OK, now you have got what not to do under your belt, it is time for a touch of hygiene homework. Here's what you have to remember to do, regularly and repeatedly. It should become second nature to you. You know you thought the

Domestic God's Do-Dos

1. Know Your Size

When cooking, select a pan of the appropriate size for your hob or stove. A small pan on a huge hob just wastes energy. Cook at a medium temperature once the liquid has boiled. Don't overfill. You are not a mad professor in the lab of a horror movie, although the results may look like it sometimes!

2. Keep a Lid on the Trash

Small can be better in lots of ways in the kitchen. If you use a small bin for your trash with matching liner rather than an industrial-sized one you could wear as a fancy dress outfit, you will take it out more regularly (that's the idea anyway). Stockpiling rubbish is smelly and dangerous. Discipline yourself.

Domestic God says ...

Keep your cool when things hot up,
wipe and polish (do your halo later).

fairies did the housework? Well, the bad news is, they don't exist. Does the truth hurt? Get over it. You always had your suspicions. It's DIY time. Focus, learn and digest. You will be tested on it later.

3. Wipe it, Swipe it

Wiping work surfaces as you dirty them is the way forward. Give them a wipe with a dishcloth dipped in hot water and detergent before and after preparing food. Don't leave food and other debris to form random, unpleasant and dangerous mosaics on the work benches. Use the right cloth, not the one closest to hand (or your socks).

4. Kitchen Captain

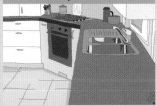

A tidy ship is a safe ship as skippers say. This motto applies to kitchens, too. As captain of the kitchen, it is your role to send below (to the cupboards at least) any equipment with no immediate task in hand. Work out what you use regularly (kettle, toaster, chopping board etc) and store the rest. It's not all hands on deck in this room.

| Technique | Tool | Wisdom | Cleaning | Chore |

Kitchen Confidential

Do you want to impress in the kitchen? Now's your chance to find out how. You have the world at your fingertips with the range of utensils available today. Amateur chefs (that means you, by the way) should take care – some items are

Use or pose: a guide to the stars

The Miniature Grater

Use

★★★
Size does matter and, in this case, small is effective. It's simply great at grating garlic and ginger.

Pose

★
What it lacks in physical dimensions on the pose front, it makes up for in ingenuity and efficiency.

The Pizza Cutter

Use

★★★★★
Cut the mustard and the pizza with this utensil. No need to rip it apart with your bare hands.

Pose

★★★★
Panache, democracy and style – you are sure to get a slice of the action with this number.

The Pepper Mill

Use

★★
It's quite a grind but big is not always best. Its size makes it better for brandishing than flavouring

Pose

★★★★★
Right up there at Numero Uno in the pose charts. Spice things up at the table in grand style.

more ostentatious than efficacious. You don't want to look like mutton dressed as lamb. Use this chart when purchasing key items. It's a sort of kitchen confidential, so keep it on a 'need to know' basis only. Don't spill the beans to everyone.

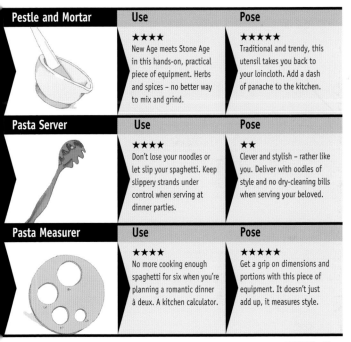

Pestle and Mortar	Use	Pose
	★★★★	★★★★★
	New Age meets Stone Age in this hands-on, practical piece of equipment. Herbs and spices – no better way to mix and grind.	Traditional and trendy, this utensil takes you back to your loincloth. Add a dash of panache to the kitchen.

Pasta Server	Use	Pose
	★★★★	★★
	Don't lose your noodles or let slip your spaghetti. Keep slippery strands under control when serving at dinner parties.	Clever and stylish – rather like you. Deliver with oodles of style and no dry-cleaning bills when serving your beloved.

Pasta Measurer	Use	Pose
	★★★★	★★★★★
	No more cooking enough spaghetti for six when you're planning a romantic dinner à deux. A kitchen calculator.	Get a grip on dimensions and portions with this piece of equipment. It doesn't just add up, it measures style.

Tools: Knives

Like many of the most important tools, knives come in a range of sizes. And just like soccer or footie players, they have individual skills. Selection for the team is based on the goals ahead and the ultimate game plan. If you are hoping

Know your Knives

Chef's Knife	Carving Knife	Serrated Bread knife

Efficient at chopping and cutting, this is an invaluable asset. Reliable, strong and a stalwart, every team should have one and play it upfront.	Indispensable for slicing thinly, this is a cutting-edge player. Good at multi-tasking, it will cut it in most line-ups. Likes a slice of the action.	A cut above the rest with bread, this knife puts tomatoes in the back of the net. Serrated, strong and serious, although a little on edge sometimes.

to score, study the game. Pick your players carefully. Can you cut it? The pre-match line-up below will help. Remember, store your knives in a wooden block or in sheaths. Don't leave them lying around or just loose in the drawer.

Sharpening Steel

Keeps everyone on their toes, a player-manager with a cutting tongue. Sharpens the action when other lose their edge. Doesn't mince words but never blunt.

Paring Knife

Skilled at peeling and other detailed manoeuvres, this is a team player but one with specific skills. Useful to have on the bench and bring out for tricky operations.

Utility Knife

Great all-rounder, likes vegetables. A valuable member of the team, it keeps the ball rolling when other players are out of action, relegated or having an early bath.

| Technique | Tool | Wisdom | Cleaning | Chore |

Tools: Pans

'Equipment is everything'. A pan manufacturer must have said that. It is a fact universally acknowledged that a man in possession of just one pan must be in need of a wee bit of advice. A man should have a range of pots and pans in the

Out of the Frying Pan ...

Small Pan

If you are melting butter or chocolate for that special sauce, boiling an egg or two to take to work the next day or making pasta sauce for two, a small pan is just fine. Don't waste energy (yours and the environment's). Small task, small pan, less washing up. More time to spend enjoying the meal.

Frying Pan

A non-stick frying pan is a must-have. You can fry anything from eggs to steak via fish, bacon, sausages, mushrooms, tomatoes, onions and garlic. Don't overdo it on the fat front though, guys. Use a dash of olive oil. Keep the temperature under control or you will have to spend time dealing with the mess.

Large Pan

Bigger culinary tasks, such as boiling pasta for several people, making soup, cooking veg etc require a larger pan. You may need to keep a lid on proceedings, so don't lose it. Put a steamer over the pan (a bamboo one or a metal 'fan') when cooking healthy veg. Keep handles facing inwards to avoid accidents.

kitchen if he is to cook up a proper storm. Read on to find out how to expand your culinary repertoire and your romantic horizons at the same time. Put a lid on this whole cooking business. Turn the heat up on your kitchen wisdom.

Casserole Dish

Casserole dishes are the best idea for cooking casseroles (funny, that) slowly in the oven. You can start the whole thing off on the hob or stove top (frying onion, garlic, browning the meat, adding the veg and the tinned tomatoes plus extra water or beer) and then relax as the stew gently cooks in the oven. It does its stuff while you do yours.

Roasting Tin

Pop your chicken, joint of meat, fillets of fish, selection of seasonal vegetables in a roasting tin, add a splash of olive oil and a handful of herbs (dried or fresh) and 'slam in the lamb', as they say. It's a versatile vessel, the roasting tin. Roast potatoes on a Sunday – what more could you want?

Wok

Woks are the sine qua non (Latin for 'gotta get me one of those') of the contemporary kitchen. You can make a speedy, healthy, tasty stir-fry at the end of a busy day at work. Great for vegetarians, great for last-minute entertaining, great for casual tête-à-tête suppers. Great all-rounders really. And they are round. Perfect.

Tools: Glasses

It is pretty transparent that a Top Executive in the Entertainment Department should bring out matching glasses at a small drinks party or formal dinner. Mishmash mismatches (try saying that after a glass or two of a nicely chilled

The Shape of Things to Come

The Big Red

Red wine glasses are generally larger than their white wine counterparts (eyes right). The curvaceous bowl allows you to swirl the wine with abandon, to release its evocative bouquet.

The Fizz Machine

Long, tall and slender, full of fizz and attractively fragile, the champagne flute is deeply romantic and glamorous. Watch the bubbles rise, clink glasses, say a few romantic words and then try to get your nose in.

The White Knight

Always hold wine glasses by the stem to avoid adding body warmth to the delicate contents. Enjoy a glass of chilled Chardonnay with your partner on a summer evening or serve a tasty Riesling before a delicious dinner.

Riesling) are OK for supper parties, but that dinner à deux with your beloved will pack more of a romantic punch if the champagne glasses are mirrors of each other, full of fizz that sparkles just a little less than your conversation.

The Social Mixer

My Name is James

The Tumbler Rumbler

If you're on a budget, buy wine glasses that suit both red and white wine and can even be used for serving water. This glass is a social chameleon and adapts to whatever is thrown at it or in it.

Now you're talking. The cocktail glass has an extraordinary glamour and resonance. Martini (shaken or stirred), olive, romance, music, sunset – what more do you need? Just buy a couple of glasses to start with – you may never need any more.

Practical, versatile, sturdy, capacious, convenient for the dishwasher (even smart enough for your favourite lager and better than the bottle, at least) – the highball is the universal glass. A tall and handsome transparent all-rounder.

Technique

Tool

Wisdom

Cleaning

Chore

The History of the Refrigerator

Way back in prehistoric times, the idea of keeping food at low temperatures had already struck Homo Erectus as a cool one. He had sussed that his freshly-caught game would last longer if kept in a cave or packed in snow. When he wasn't in the mood for hunter-gathering or the open-air market was looking a bit down on stocks, he could dine from his personal cooler. Mr Erectus kick-started the notion of keeping things cool in order to preserve them, but it was quite some time before his cannier descendants harvested ice from lakes and rivers or manufactured and stored it.

On chilly nights the Egyptians and Indians would prepare ice by placing earthenware pots outside, filled with water. Food in the 18th century was kept chilled in ice houses, with sheets of ice packed in salt, wrapped in fabric and stored below ground. The verb 'to refrigerate' comes from the Latin word for frost (*frigus*) but it was never declined in Latin, first being heard around the middle of the 16th century according to some, or coined in 1800 by an American engineer according to others. The first known artificial refrigeration was demonstrated at the University of Glasgow in 1748, but it was not until 1805 that an American inventor, Oliver Evans designed the first refrigeration machine.

Mass production of modern refrigerators hit the domestic market after the Second World War and transformed life for the cook, the shopper, the diner and the butcher. Today, it would be hard to imagine life without one. How would you keep your beer chilled or your champagne on ice? What a nightmare thought! Instead of going to the supermarket, you would have to park near a stream and lift out your chilled foods. Or go into a dark cellar and retrieve your ice cream from a large, unwieldy box (perhaps you do that anyway!)

Refrigerators and freezers are heat pumps – they move heat energy from cold (low-temperature) areas to hot (high-temperature) ones, against its natural flow, thereby increasing the coldness of the cold areas. They compress a substance called a refrigerant and allow it to expand. Early models used ammonia to do this but we use different substances but the same process today.

Refrigerators demand care. Their's is a tough job. Respect that.

Keeping it Cool

When did you last see your refrigerator naked with the lights on? Has it been a while? If so, it's time to change things. Once a season, at least, strip your refrigerator bare and give it a thorough going over, unplugging it before you embark on the mission.

A cool, clean refrigerator can help you get the most freshness, taste and nutrition from its contents. You may think that cold equals clean, but although the temperature may be very low, some bacteria manage to survive and create food safety problems. Remove the shelves and wash both sides thoroughly with hot, soapy water. Start at the top of the refrigerator to avoid having to start all over again. Get rid of all the spills, mould and mildew. You can use a paste of bicarbonate of soda and water (four tablespoons of each) to clean the inside. This will also help eliminate stale smells. A dish of charcoal left overnight helps to remove any obstinate odours. Rinse with a damp cloth, dry with a clean one. Clean the door (inside and out), the seals and the handle. Take the opportunity to evict squatters – food well past its eat-by date, shrivelled leftovers, anything sporting unfashionable mould and items that were in there untouched last time you cleaned the refrigerator. Don't forget to put the plug back in the socket!

 Domestic God

Keep your refrigerator well stocked. Score on every level.

I'm too cool for my kitchen

Today, refrigerators can keep track of their own contents, connect to your computer and place orders directly online without you stirring from your bed. Some come equipped with televisions, cameras, water dispensers, ice makers, and facilities for dishing out recipes, nutritional information and e-mails. The only downside is, they can't self-clean. Your role is to invent one that can, or do the job yourself. Think of the refrigerator as your inbox of e-mails – old messages are stale or potentially damaging. They overflow, get blocked and can contaminate. Sensible, safe storage – that's the most obvious answer.

Cool Facts

Don't Overload

- Don't overload the refrigerator. Proper air circulation equals proper refrigeration. And you will be able to find things more easily.

- Put the new container of milk behind the one already in the refrigerator to avoid cheesy milk lurking at the back.

- Don't keep opening the door – it increases both the temperature and your waist measurement.

Thermometer

- Invest in a refrigerator thermometer (they cost less than a beer) to alert you to any temperature problems. Put it in the middle of the unit and check every week. The temperature should be at least four degrees celsius or lower.

- Heat rises (remember your school days?) so the coolest part is likely to be at the bottom of the unit or at the back of the shelf.

- Keep meats, fish, poultry and milk at the bottom of the fridge.

Temperature

- The temperature in the door will fluctuate most due to frequent opening. Use it for pickles, salad dressings, condiments, soft drinks, beer and wine rather than milk and eggs and products most sensitive to temperature changes.

- Give your refrigerator a spring clean every season, plus a good wipe every week and when you put your new shopping in.

Special Compartments

- If your model has special compartments for cheese, meats, fruit and vegetables, use them for the products for which they are designed, except for the egg holder. Throw this away or use it as a mould for homemade candles or a foot spa for a pet tarantula. Keep eggs on the main shelf in the shop carton – that is where they belong. Use them within four weeks of purchase.

- Cover food before refrigerating and store raw foods below cooked foods.

- Promptly cool and eat any leftovers.

Keeping Things on Ice

A freezer is not a long-term storage solution, like a cupboard under the stairs with a plug or a trunk with electricity in a rarely visited attic. Good freezing or Nice Ice is having useful stocks of frozen supplies for last-minute or much-planned invitations back to your place, cook-from-frozen emergency meals with your mother or unexpected(ly) romantic breakfasts. If your mother makes a delicious casserole one Sunday lunch when you are round there, take a little home in a proper freezer-proof container, write the contents and date on it and put in the freezer for an evening of football or the Eurovision Song Contest.

Bad freezing or Ice Vice is an ice sculpture food mountain destined for the bin not the pan, due to lack of official ID and the danger of being of pensionable age.

UFOs

Don't overload your freezer. Identify each item with a label showing contents and date of entry (not necessary for packaged, labelled foods). UFOs (unidentifiable frozen objects) should be treated without mercy. You don't know how long they have been in there or even what they contain. Freeze in small quantities rather than large ones . Never refreeze foods once they have thawed out. After purchase, take frozen food home quickly and put straight in the freezer (unless you are going to eat it that day, in which case put it in the refrigerator). Don't leave it in your rucksack or briefcase or under the desk at work. Put a cool bag or cool box on your birthday wish list.

Keep fresh or frozen meat, fish and poultry in its original wrapping. You might want to put food in a plastic bag if you plan to keep it in the freezer for more than two months. Make sure food is stored in containers that are both air- and moisture-proof. The temperature should be minus 18 degrees celsius or below. Allow meat, poultry and fish to defrost slowly in the refrigerator or defrost in a microwave. Once thawed, refrigerate for up to 24 hours or cook immediately. You can then refreeze.

Keep it on ice

Coffee kept in the freezer stays fresh longer. Always have some in stock for unplanned lazy mornings spent with your beloved. Freeze some croissants and bagels to go with it. Keep some bacon or smoked salmon on ice, too, if they take your fancy, but not eggs.

Should you find yourself in possession of leftover white and red wine, pour it into an ice tray and you will always have small amounts on hand for sauces.

Put a mint leaf or a raspberry in each compartment of the ice tray before filling with water. Drop nonchalantly into a cocktail glass to impress at parties.

Try to store the basics for a 'cook-from-frozen' meal for two, four or six people (depending on how popular you are) for short-notice entertaining or one of those unplanned late-night invitations of the 'everybody come back to my place for something to eat' kind.

Defrosting Tips

Ideally, you should defrost food in the refrigerator, in cold running water or in the microwave. Take care to defrost thoroughly.

- Plan ahead and thaw food in the refrigerator, where it will remain at a safe and constant temperature. It takes longer but is safer.

- If you are planning to roast a big turkey, for example, allow a day (24 hours) in the fridge to thaw. Even a chicken breast takes a day, so take it out the night before you plan to cook it, and when you get back from work it will be ready.

- Once thawed in the refrigerator, ground meat and poultry should be OK for a day before cooking.

- If you are thawing under cold water, ensure the package is leak-proof or

bacteria from the air or area around it could be introduced into the food. Submerge the bag in cold tap water and keep changing the water every half hour. Small packages of about 2kg should take about an hour. Once thawed properly, cook immediately.

- If you defrost in the microwave, cook immediately as some areas may start to cook while defrosting.

- If your food gets freezer burn, don't worry. Cut the relevant part off before cooking. It has dried out, that's all.

- When reheating cooked food cook it until it is steaming hot throughout. Kill those pesky bacteria.

Good Refrigerator/Bad Refrigerator

Open your refrigerator and compare its contents to a work of art. A minimalist, two-tone canvas by an artist working in cardboard and aluminium? Or a luscious portrayal of nature's produce interspersed with the best of 21st-century manmade products? Ask yourself if you could make an impromptu meal with its contents? If you were feeling unwell and unable to go out for a few days, could you survive

✖ Bad Refrigerator

Bad refrigerators can be almost empty, except for the leftovers of takeouts and a lonely can of beer, or almost full to bursting, groaning with food that belongs in a laboratory, vegetables that are limp and slimy, milk that has serious BO, cheese that is overwhelming its neighbours with its pungency (intentional or accidental), open cans of congealed beans or rice pudding. Unintentionally green is bad. The coolest fridge mentality is somewhere between stock and siege. Bad refrigerators have few (if any) of the following: fresh milk, butter or margarine, eggs, fruit, veg, fish and meat (optional). They provide no nourishment. They are full of food well beyond its natural life. Their owners are not cool investigators. They don't check dates on supplies frequently, they don't monitor the temperature, ventilation or hygiene.

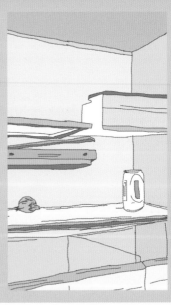

Domestic God says ...

Cool, accessible, hygienic, everything in the right place...you and the fridge.

Dirty Devil says ...

Barely approachable, empty of inspiration, unhygienic and unhealthy...you and the fridge

on what you have stored in the refrigerator? Just how many vitamins could you identify and enjoy munching on the food inside? If the answers are no, not really and none, you will know which category (and takeout trap) you fall into.

✓ Good Refrigerator

Good refrigerators have cool operators, keenly aware of the nutritional value and vitamin content of their supplies together with their ETA and ETD (estimated time of arrival and departure), freshness and life expectancy. Food is in the compartment specially designed for it. Eggs sit proudly on the shelf and not in the door. The door is opened only when necessary and then closed firmly. Its shelves are cleaned regularly with soapy water. Leftovers are removed after two to three days. Milk spends a week tops in there – not a month. Butter meets Bin after eight weeks max. Pungent cheeses and seafood are wrapped to avoid BO contagion. There are no half-empty or even half-full cans. Everything carries an ID. It is counted in and counted out. Cool, eh?

What's in Store

Maintaining a well-stocked larder is a vital strategy for men in complete or even partial charge of the kitchen. Just think, our cavemen ancestors benefited from having the largest organic open-air market known to man right outside their

Larder Perfection

Let's identify the canned foods that you should try to keep in stock in the larder so you can cook a meal without needing to get extra supplies:

MUST HAVES
- Fish (tuna, sardines, salmon, crab)
- Vegetables (tomatoes, sweetcorn, asparagus, beans, peas, chick peas)
- Fruit (peaches, apples, pears, raspberries, etc.)
- Soup (the usual suspects – tomato, chicken, clam chowder, pumpkin – plus lobster bisque for a special occasion)
- Custard, rice pudding (great comfort food)

ADD THESE
- Stock Cubes (for sauces and gravy)

dwellings (OK, so they did have to hunt and gather for the privilege). Nowadays the club and spear have been replaced by the somewhat less macho but often more reliable shopping trolley and credit card.

- Olive oil (for dressings)
- Sunflower oil (for stir fries)
- Vinegar (balsamic, red and white wine, and cheap vinegar for washing windows!)
- Mustard, pickles and other condiments
- Salt and pepper
- Herbs, spices and curry powder
- Tomato ketchup, paste, purée and sauces
- Soy sauce, teriyaki sauce, fish sauce, coconut milk (for Asian dishes)
- Tabasco sauce, Worcestershire sauce
- Pesto sauce (for pasta)
- Honey
- Peanut butter
- Jams, marmalade and jellies
- Chocolate (to melt over ice cream)

- Coffee, tea and cocoa
- Sherry, Madeira and Marsala (for sauces)

STAPLES
- Pasta, rice, noodles (don't ever run out!)
- Couscous (for more adventurous cuisine)
- Dried beans, lentils and other pulses
- Flour
- Bicarbonate of soda (for stains and odours!)
- Baking powder
- Breakfast cereals (healthy and low in sugar)
- Dried fruit (for office snacks and baking)
- Olives (for cocktails and pasta sauces)
- Crisps, crackers and pretzels (for guests)
- Cheese biscuits (for dinner parties)
- Sugar (brown and white)

- Condensed or long-life milk (for emergencies and some desserts)

ADVENTUROUS STAPLES
- Polenta
- Japanese udon, soba and ramen noodles
- Refried beans
- Bamboo shoots
- Jar of roasted red peppers

HAVE TO HAND
- Potatoes – store in a cool, dark place
- Onions (red and white) and garlic – don't store in refrigerator – invest in a wire basket
- Tomatoes – keep in a bowl on the kitchen counter
- Lemons and limes (for cocktails)

Food Facts

Imagine your body is an expensive, finely tuned sports car – you obviously want it to run on the best fuel available, right? The food pyramid below shows all the main food groups: you should eat more of the power foods at the base and less of those at the top. You know it makes sense!

It's all in the Balance

A balanced diet is important for long-term health and includes a combination of several different food types: grains and pulses; fresh fruit and vegetables; meat, fish and dairy products; fats, oils and sweets. The right balance allows you to maintain a healthy weight and get essential nutrients, such as fatty acids, proteins for repair and regeneration, and vitamins and minerals. A proper diet helps look after your heart and arteries, boost immunity and reduce the risk of certain cancers.

Go very easy on the foods at the top of the pyramid (left). Enjoy moderate amounts of the protein-rich foods and dairy items and minimize their fat content by trimming fat off meat and resisting chicken skin. The way food is prepared is also a factor – go for grilling rather than frying, unless it's a low-fat stir fry. Dump the breadcrumbs, batter and pastry.

Five Alive

Don't be a banana, eat one. You should consume at least five portions of fruit and vegetables a day. They are an excellent source of vitamins, minerals and fibre – and free of cholesterol. If you get a snack attack, eat an apple or a handful of dried fruit or nuts. When the object of your heart's desire in the office offers you a sweet, resist temptation.

Get Fresh

OK, so you don't have the time or energy to get fresh every day, but a regular diet of processed, ready-made food and takeouts is not good for you. Try to eat fresh, organic (if possible), seasonal food as much as your schedule and budget will allow. Food doesn't have to be cooked. Sushi, for example, is a delicious, healthy option at lunchtime, while raw oysters are an aphrodisiac.

Waiter, More Water Please

Drink alcohol in moderation and designate a number of alcohol-free days every week. Remember how good it feels the next day. Make an effort to drink more water, in between alcoholic drinks and in general. If you do regular exercise, it is important to replenish fluid. And while you are thinking about it, go easy on caffeinated drinks.

| Technique | Tool | Wisdom | Cleaning | Chore |

Carving a Whole Chicken

Once you have mastered carving, you will want to do it in front of your guests. A couple of test runs are a good idea. Rehearse with housemates before doing a live performance. Sometimes it's cool to be chicken in order to avoid looking a turkey.

Remove the chicken from the oven, place on a carving board and cover loosely with foil. Allow to 'rest' for about 15 minutes. This allows the juices to sink into the flesh, resulting in plump, moist meat. Place the bird on a carving board with a well to catch the juices and remove any trussing strings. Spoon any stuffing into a serving dish and keep warm. Use any juices for pan-gravy.

Nice Slicing

1	2	3

Using a carving knife (or an electric one if you haven't been to the gym for a few days), cut through the skin between the thigh and body.	Continue cutting until you reach the ball-and-socket joint, then twist the leg away from the body. Cut the drumstick and thigh apart.	Hold the drumstick upright, at a convenient angle to the plate and cut down, turning the drumstick in order to get uniform slices.

Leftover laws

Put leftover turkey or chicken in the refrigerator as soon as possible, removing the flesh from the bones first. Don't leave the carcass in DINING ROOM overnight – the meat needs to get back into the refrigerator within a couple of hours. Eat the leftovers within three days maximum. You can freeze sliced turkey or chicken (put it in a proper storage container), but do use it within one month or evict it from the house. Remember the UFO theory (see page 40).

4

Hold thigh firmly on plate with a fork, and cut slices of meat parallel to the bone.

5

Cut off the wing. Carve the other side. Arrange the wings and slices on the serving plate. Smile. Make a deep cut into the breast close to the wing.

6

Beginning at the front, halfway up the breast, cut thin slices of white meat.

Mission accomplished. Await applause from impressed and hungry guests.

Technique

Tool

Wisdom

Cleaning

Chore

Making a Cocktail

Like you, cocktails are fashionable, stylish and glamorous. Think interesting combinations, unexpected unions and a dash of danger. Think shaken, not stirred. Think Bond. Be a good social mixer.

Cocktails

Any self-respecting barman has a certain amount of equipment and knows how to use it in front of an audience. Keys to success include a stylish cocktail shaker, an ice bucket, interesting glassware, a jigger (measure), lots of crushed ice and an understanding of both timing and performance – and don't forget straws and umbrellas. Depending on which cocktail(s) you decide to make, you will need a good supply of the relevant liquor(s), spirits, soda, tonic, fruit juices, cream, olives, limes and sickly-sweet glacé cherries. The good news is that at cocktail parties you generally don't need to feed your guests. Nuts and crisps are fine.

Shake, Rattle or Roll?

Different cocktails demand different skills. Brush up on who likes what (and to which recipe) so you can impress your guests.

The Perfect Buck's Fizz

In 1921, a certain Mr McGarry of Buck's Club in London felt suddenly inspired to mix one part orange juice with two parts chilled champagne and add a dash of grenadine. The Buck's Fizz was born. Although a simple affair, it is glamorous and evocative, perfect for getting a dinner party or a sunny Sunday morning with your beloved off to a good start. Serve in a fluted glass and wait for the bubbles to rise (you can fake it with sparkling wine or Cava instead). If you don't finish the whole bottle, don't worry – it will retain its bubbles overnight in the refrigerator without a stopper (or a silver spoon).

| Technique | Tool | Wisdom | Cleaning | Chore |

Whose Turn to Wash the Dishes?

There's no denying that washing the dishes is up there with ironing on the list of least popular household activities. However, in the interests of hygiene it is a must. You can't eat from paper plates or pizza boxes forever.

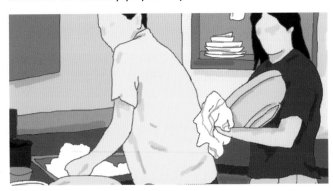

Hot and Bubbly

1 FILL YOUR BOWL

Fill your bowl or sink with hot water (doh – not right to the top) and add detergent – check the instructions and don't go overboard. If you put on protective plastic gloves, you'll be able to use really hot water, which is more hygienic and cleans more deeply; cool is not cool for dirt and debris.

2 LOVELY BUBBLY

Now it's time to sink your hands into those lovely clean bubbles. Wash the glasses first, one by one if they are your best wine or champagne glasses given to you by a beloved aunt. Cutlery comes next, then china, followed by large bowls and dishes. Pots and pans dive in last. You may need to change the water in between if it gets very dirty or if all the suds vanish.

Soak and destroy

Try to reserve the kitchen sink for food-related activities only, as other household mess can bring about germ transfer. Don't risk cross-contamination with cloths – use dishcloths for washing dishes and tea towels for drying them. Don't even think about using a floor cloth for either mission. It's a good idea to clean up your pots, pans, bowls and worksurfaces as you go. Paper towels are good for mopping up spills and don't spread germs, since they are disposable.

Don't forget – we are never alone. Pests love dirty dishes that, if left for any length of time, become smelly. Soon bacteria multiply then invite their friends round for a leftovers party. Worse still, ants and cockroaches may gatecrash. If you can't wash-up last minute items before serving food, fill them with hot water (plus

detergent if they're greasy) and allow to soak until after the meal.

Pans with really stubborn food residues can be left to soak overnight, or you can fill them with water, add detergent and allow the leftovers to simmer on the heat. The food will loosen gradually and you can then wash up as normal. To clean a scorched pan, fill with water, add a few tablespoons of bicarbonate of soda and boil until the scorched parts come loose. Don't leave the room during this process.

Domestic God says ...

Just 30 minutes of moderately vigorous activity at the sink burns off about 80 calories. If all goes well, more calories could be worked off a Domestic God later.

3 FLEX THE PECS

Wash the dishes with a cloth, sponge or brush and flex your biceps slightly but not excessively, particularly if you have serious muscle tone. A circular motion works well. If you have to use an abrasive scourer for stubborn stains, use the appropriate one for the surface or you will damage it. Be very gentle with non-stick pans; treat them like your partner – with respect and care.

4 RINSING IS RIGHT

Rinse all items in hot, clean water. This follow-up action has a number of advantages – hygienic (it destroys more germs), aesthetic (it prevents streaking) and strategic (it accelerates the drying process). And when you next have a glass of champagne, it means only the right bubbles will fizz and float to the surface. Rinsing is right, so go for it.

Taking the Heat in the Kitchen

Come on guys, the oven may not be a page-turner of a subject, but there is some good news to keep you going – three little words in fact (or four without a hyphen) – they are The Self-Cleaning Oven. What could be simpler? All you have to do is read the manual and get out of the kitchen when things get a bit hot. For other appliances and surfaces, you may need a bit more effort though.

Although they cook as if by magic, microwave ovens require a magician's assistant to keep them clean and in full working order. Food often makes a mess when cooked in a microwave. Check the manufacturer's instructions for methods and cleaning products but a quick daily (OK, twice-weekly) wipe with warm water and a mild detergent should suffice. Don't use a commercial oven cleaner or the magic tricks may go horribly wrong.

Remove the circular plate and wash in the sink, removing all food deposits. Wash the interior of the microwave, its sides, door (inside and out) and seals.

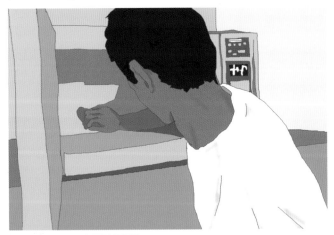

Reheat a Takeout

Ideally, a takeout should be eaten while still hot. If you decide to eat it later, cover and refrigerate it immediately. Use within one day, reheat it only once and ensure it is served piping hot. You may not be able to see or smell germs, but they are cunning little critters and masters of disguise.

1. Wash hands in hot, soapy water for at least ten seconds. This is an excellent house rule, by the way, for all food preparation.

2. Transfer food into a ceramic or glass dish. Aluminium foil containers must not be placed in a microwave oven.

3. Cover food with a microwave-safe lid or plastic wrap, taking care that it does not come into direct contact with the food.

4. Halfway through the calculated cooking time, open the door, stir the dish, replace the cover and continue.

5. The bell will sound, indicating it is time to remove the food. Wait for at least 60 seconds before serving.

6. Deodorize the microwave after use by putting a bowl of water with a slice or two of lemon on high for a couple of minutes. A sneaky, squeaky clean piece of kitchen towel on the microwave turntable minimizes spills.

Washing Floors and Windows

Regular vacuuming preserves both your carpet's quality and appearance but why not try to minimize dirt in the first place. Use a dirt-trapping doormat at the front door or entrance to the room and rugs or runners in the hallway. Ask people to wipe or remove shoes and boots at the front door.

Move the furniture periodically (lift not push please) to avoid permanent crushing. Use castors and protectors under furniture legs to prevent squashing the pile. A handy hint that really works for removing dents is to place an ice cube in each one. As the cube melts the fibres swell. Run over the dents with a vacuum cleaner and the wet fibres will become upright again. Neat uh?

Natural is nice

Many people opt for natural floor coverings such as sisal, jute or coir nowadays. They are hardwearing alternatives and work well in households with small two-legged or four-legged inhabitants. They should be vacuumed regularly (the floors, not the children or pets) and on both sides if they are rugs (again not the children or pets). Stains are less obvious on such floorings, but that doesn't mean you can leave them. To remove mud or other solids, lift off the excess with care and leave the rest to dry. Brush along the weave with a stiff brush and then vacuum. Liquid spills should be dealt with swiftly. Blot

firmly, working from the outside in. Avoid wetting the area further and don't even think of using a conventional carpet shampoo. For persistent stains, call in the professionals.

Cork floors

If you have a cork floor, take extra care. Vacuum or sweep regularly but resist the temptation to rush off and get the mop and

Solid Hardwood Floors

DIRT, GRIT AND SAND will scratch, dent and dull your floors. Invest in floor mats and keep floors clean. Sweep regularly using a broom equipped with fine ends that can trap the dirt effectively.

PETS with long nails and weak bladders scratch and stain wood. Train your pets and trim their claws (sadly, felt pads don't work on dogs and cats).

LIQUID SPILLS (water, coffee, wine, etc) left for any length of time on the floor will cause stains. Wipe up spills as soon as they happen.

LADIES with high heels and dangerous stilettos can leave an impression on you and your floor. Ask them politely to remove their perilous footwear – everyone will feel more comfortable.

bucket. Remember, cork floors are made from the cork tree and are therefore organic. They need to be cleaned with appropriate specialist liquids and waxes. Ask your local hardware store to advise you. Always deal with spills as soon as they occur. You may well prevent the formation of stains by so doing. Act now, no need to repent later.

Linoleum floors

Linoleum is becoming increasingly popular. Made with linseed oil, ground cork, wood, flour and resins, it is quite environmentally sound while being comfortable and warm. Amazingly enough, it is also able to destroy bacteria on the floor naturally, leaving you with less work. Cleaning is easy. Just sweep and vacuum thoroughly (but not aggressively) before washing with detergent and warm water.

Rugs

Rugs are a great idea for the living area. They can introduce colour to the room while protecting the floor from heavy traffic. Anchoring a rug to the floor using a non-slip felt mat equipped with an adhesive base will keep it safely in place. Rugs don't escape attack by nasty critters and need to be vacuumed regularly.

Windows on the world

Dusting or vacuuming your window frames and sills regularly is important for their maintenance. Give the paint a wash every month if you can. Think of your windows as the eyes of your home onto the outside world. Light has to filter through the same obstacles in order to enter the room, affecting both its mood and your own. Dirty windows never make a good impression.

| Technique | Tool | Wisdom | Cleaning | Chore |

Washing and Wiping

Regular dusting and vacuuming of walls and ceilings helps keep them in good condition and makes the 'big spring clean' less daunting, arduous and time-consuming. Use the long brush attachment on your vacuum for the ceiling, applying the principle of top to bottom, high to low. Failure to embrace this strategy will result in a temper-testing duplication of the task.

Wall to Wall

ESSENTIAL EQUIPMENT:

- A vacuum cleaner to remove dust from ceiling and walls.
- A strong and reliable ladder or a high stool.
- A bucket of mild all-purpose detergent diluted in water and a second bucket of clean water.
- A clean cloth (or sponge) x three.
- A partner (existing rather than potential), or friend

Wall care

Before you start, check that your paintwork is indeed washable. Most painted surfaces are fine, but washing can damage some emulsion paints. Always test-clean a patch (avoiding obvious areas) using diluted detergent and allow to dry. You may decide to repaint surfaces unsuitable for washing.

Wash the ceiling and walls in manageable chunks, using energetic, circular motions, remembering to wring the cloths well at each stage. Always rinse with a clean cloth and dry with another equally pristine one. The top-to-bottom rule applies here too.

Many wallpapers are washable and the same instructions apply if so, but motions should be more gentle and you must pat the paper dry at the end with a clean, dry cloth. Vacuuming or dusting them first is important and a preliminary test wash of an inconspicuous patch is a good idea, just to be on the safe side.

Up against the wall

Don't forget to remove grubby fingerprints from light switches and their surrounds. Dirty marks on the walls around switches can be removed using a soft eraser.

Try spot-cleaning painted or papered surfaces with specific chemical products (read instructions carefully).

Remove cobwebs from walls regularly. They are unsightly and you wouldn't want one to land suddenly on top of your partner's mother, would you? Wrong answer!

Kitchen walls need washing more frequently than those in other rooms. They are in direct contact with steam, grease, sticky fingers and graffiti artists on a daily basis. If your walls are really greasy, wash them down with a solution of sugar soap. It cuts its way through grime and prepares the surface for repainting. Don't be tempted to just paint over dirty walls – it is not the right solution.

If you have wall hangings, give them a good shake from time to time to disturb any moths enjoying free accommodation behind them.

Wall-to-wall partying

Have a wall-washing party – invite a few friends round and tell them it is a BYOB affair (Bring your own Bucket). You provide the beers and the music. It will be done in a flash. Don't attempt wall washing with a hangover or if you suffer from vertigo. Beware of inviting ex-lovers or neighbours bearing grudges as well as red wine and a bucket.

| Technique | Tool | Wisdom | Cleaning | Chore |

Stain Removal

Stains are inevitable within the home, however much care you may take to prevent them, but the quicker you act, the more successful you are likely to be at removing them. Deal, don't disguise. Heal, don't hide.

Stain Removal Kit (SRK)

Every household needs a Stain Removal Kit (SRK) primed for action at any moment. For general household incidents, the following equipment is all you need. Photocopy the list and take it to the store:

- ABSORBENT PAPER TOWELS OR SPONGES
- CLEAN, ABSORBENT WHITE CLOTHS
- ALL-PURPOSE DETERGENT
- WHITE VINEGAR
- WHITE SPIRIT
- BLEACH
- AMMONIA
- NON-OILY NAIL VARNISH REMOVER
- LAUNDRY STAIN PRE-TREATMENT PRODUCT
- SPECIALIST STAIN REMOVERS (FOR THINGS LIKE BALLPOINT OR FELT-TIP STAINS)
- RUBBING ALCOHOL
- BICARBONATE OF SODA
- SOLVENT-TYPE CLEANING FLUIDS OR DRY-CLEANING FLUIDS
- NON-SOLVENT STAIN OR SPOT REMOVER
- LEMONS

FLOORS

Before you set about removing stains from wood flooring, it is important to ascertain if the stain or scratch is in the wood itself or on the topcoat finish.

NATURAL- OR WAX-FINISH FLOORS / FLOORS WITHOUT HARD FINISHES Gently rub the stain with a damp cloth, rub dry and then wax. Again, the working-from-outside-in principle applies. Water stains should be rubbed with steel wool and then waxed. White rings can be removed using a paste of salt and olive oil left on the stain overnight. Wipe off the next morning and re-wax.

WOOD FLOORS WITH HARD FINISHES OR VARNISHES, INCLUDING POLYURETHANE Care needs to be taken with such floors (you can detect them by checking to see if the stain is in the superficial finish). Scratches should be repaired with specialist kits available from flooring retailers and other stains should be treated with specialist cleaners for urethane finishes.

Removing a Stain

1	**2**	**3**	**4**
Don't waste time. Grab some paper towel and act. Pulling a rug over the stain won't help. Ignoring it won't make it go away. It's like toothache. Think SBS – scoop, blot, solution. If it's a liquid spill, it's more of a BBS – blot, blot solution technique. Blot with paper towel or a soft, clean and colourfast cloth.	If the spill is solid or semi-solid, you need to scoop up as much of it as you can with a spoon, spatula or similar blunt object. Don't use a carving knife – cutting out a stain is not a solution. Be careful to contain the spill. Don't play with it or rub it into the carpet. This is serious stuff and you need to get a grip.	Now is the time to apply the cleaning substance. Use a mixture of detergent and water or a specialist stain remover. Read the instructions. It's a good idea to do a test patch first in an inconspicuous spot. Apply the cleaning substance directly to the stain, give it time to do its work and then blot clean.	The final tactic is to spray lukewarm water over the offending area and blot as usual. Once the carpet is dry, gently brush or vacuum the area to restore its pile and glory. You may need to repeat this process. If you fancy steam- or dry-cleaning your carpets, call in the professionals.

WALLS AND PAINTWORK

Unwanted scribbling on the walls calls for bicarbonate of soda diluted with a little water in a small bowl to form a thick paste. Rub gently on the offending mark.

Stain removal on wallpaper is a tricky business and you may end up making things worse. Choose from a wide selection of commercial substances, including solvents, but follow instructions carefully and check they are safe for your type of wallpaper. Sometimes, rubbing dirty patches with stale white bread has been known to work (who said household management was predictable).

Plant an Idea

Think of your home as a mini-earth, equipped with a range of different climatic conditions. Your kitchen is more like a steamy jungle than any other rooms in the house and usually gets lots of direct sunlight. You need to see plants not as isolated, pretty objects that bring a spot of colour or scent to your home, but as part of the living domestic ecosystem. Your job as an indoor gardener is to create mini-ecosystems that provide sufficient light, water, food and warmth and choose the plants that suit those conditions.

The kitchen is a very popular place for indoor plants and suits most species, among them Cacti, Succulents, Hyacinths and Pelargoniums. Lighting is usually bright and the air moist, and these conditions suit a number of plants.

Choose with care

Don't buy the first pretty plant you come across. Check the temperature, humidity, intensity and direction of light in your kitchen and then take a look at the plant suitability tag or ask the retailer for advice. Choose a plant with clean, healthy-looking foliage and no signs of pest, disease or discoloration.

Rule of thumb

To detect when to water, press your thumb into the soil to test moisture content and only water when it feels dry. If the soil loses touch with the sides of the container, you left it rather late. To revive a dehydrated plant, loosen the top layer of soil to allow the water to permeate to the roots. Water the plant thoroughly and spray the leaves with tepid water.

Cleaning leaves

Yes, houseplants involve housework, but not too much. Dust is dangerous. It not only spoils the appearance of your plant but it also blocks the leaf's

pores and restricts its breathing. It blocks out light and may contain harmful chemicals. Hardy plants with glossy leaves, such as the Rubber Plant, can be cleaned by sponging the leaves with soapy water. Smaller plants need gentle treatment and should not be cleaned with liquid or chemicals. Use a soft brush to lightly dust the surface. Don't wash or polish young leaves.

Handle with care

Watering is key to caring for your houseplant. Too much water and the root system will be unable to breathe, causing yellowed leaves, rot and death. Too little water and the plant will also die. Use tepid water for plant watering. Pour enough water onto the top of the soil for surplus to accumulate in the pot in which the plant is standing. Do not let the plant stand in this water for any length of time. The warmer the room, the greater the evaporation and the more water your plant will require.

Get green fingers

Herbs look, smell and taste good and you don't need to be too much of a gardener to keep them flourishing in pots in the kitchen. Chives, basil, thyme and mint do well indoors, and you can keep them in separate pots or put them in a single, longer container. This prevents them becoming pot-bound and helps the humidity and soil moisture to remain more even. Herbs just love the sun, so north-facing windows are not ideal and less than four hours a day of sunlight doesn't suit them. Remember to water them,

but not too much. Pinch out the basil leaves and put them over your fresh pasta or salad. Add some freshly-chopped chives to your omelette, chop some mint and put in a ramekin (or clean jam jar), add a tablespoon of boiling water, a teaspoon of

vinegar and a pinch of sugar and voilà, your own mint sauce for lamb chops. Try some fresh herbs on the windowsill. They will come in handy for cooking and add a professional touch to your image and cuisine. Don't splash with hot, soapy water.

Petiquette in the Kitchen

Pets are wonderful things. Medical studies have shown that they keep us healthy and calm. Cats and dogs (and fish too – who knows?) are always delighted to see you. However, with a pet come additional responsibilities. Suddenly, it is not all about you and your partner or housemate any more. The pitter-patter of tiny feet covered in mud and carrying things into the kitchen from the road, field or backyard can be heard in every room. Watch out in particular in the kitchen. There are already quite a number of bacterial exchanges at play in this room. Don't add to them.

If you have to leave your pet while you go to work, make sure that you know which rooms Felix or Rover will be in. A few house rules need to be established. If you leave your kitchen full of tempting food, dangerous plugs and cords and the TV remote control just a hop, skip and a jaw-bite away, you will not be as happy to see your pet when you return as he or she is to see you. Remember, a large, excitable dog in a tiny apartment is not a love match.

Helpful Hygiene

- Keep your pet away from the food preparation zone and don't encourange begging at the table.

- Wash your hands after stroking your pet and don't touch your eyes or handle food before your hands are absolutely clean.

- Try to limit your pet to certain rooms in the house and establish one pet-free zone. Keep your pet clean by regularly brushing and washing.

- Each to their own: don't share bowls or plates with your pet. Buy your pet an attractive bowl and make sure everyone in the house uses it for Rover or Felix.

- Check the kitchen before you leave the house for anything that could harm your pet.

✓ Do-Dos

Invest in your Pet
A wise investment generally leads to dividends. Consider it a 'petfolio.' Spend time with your pet each day, buy it toys and chews, install a padded perch near a sunny window for your cat or a comfortable place for your dog to relax. Plant cat grass in indoor pots for your feline friend so it can graze. Buy a ready-made cat tree for climbing opportunities. A happy pet is more likely to be a safe one.

Breed Needs
Do some serious research about the breed of dog that suits your circumstances. How much space, time and energy can you devote to it?

Think about the pet rather than yourself when you do this. Dogs are portrayed in the media as ornaments, trophies and fashion statements. If this is what you want, get a battery-operated pet.

✗ No-Nos

Fish deserve Respect
A goldfish bowl is only a temporary home for Goldie – his or her (how do you tell?) permanent address should be a correct-sized aquarium complete with plants, a pump and toys, etc. Clean it once a month, don't overfeed Goldie and, if you use tap water, check if chemicals need to be added to remove the chlorine.

Fire, Flames and Fur
Never leave your pet alone in a room with a lit candle or an unattended fire. Animals are attracted to the bright lights and can knock the candles over, spilling hot wax onto the carpet and themselves, and creating a fire hazard.

Boney Bits
Be wary of giving your pets the leftovers of a roast dinner. Chicken bones can be lethal for cats and dogs.

Bug Off

Bugs, germs and bacteria. Foodborne, airborne, newborn, reborn. You
have to contend with all of these in the kitchen. Silent, invisible, deadly.
Sound familiar? In this case, we are talking BUG. It stands for butt-ugly
germ. Ever seen a weevil on the catwalk, a bacteria to-die-for (rather than
-of), a campylobacter in a bikini? Here are some other models to think about –
E. Coli 0157, Listeria, Salmonella, Clostridium Perfingens. Now you have been
introduced, don't get involved and learn how to dump them heartlessly.

Bug Facts

- Bacteria enter the body through the digestive system and so this is where the symptoms concentrated – nausea, vomiting, cramps and diarrhoea. You know the score.

- Bacteria need warmth and moisture to grow and reproduce simply by dividing themselves. They are called bacterium in the singular, but they don't stay on the shelf for long.

- One becomes two, two become four, four become a million between you going to bed and waking up. It's maths gone crazy like a great day on Wall Street.

- Say you leave food out of the fridge overnight, the next morning you will be entering a seriously contaminated zone. One quick mouthful and you could be very ill. Refrigerate or evacuate to eliminate. Don't give them a chance.

- Keep cooked and uncooked meats apart. Wash your hands if you plan to handle both. Cross-contamination makes you just that – cross and contaminated.

- Use different chopping boards for cooked and uncooked meats and a different one for vegetables. Scrub thoroughly after use.

- Reheat food to 75°C (167°F) to kill bacteria. Dead.

Mould, Mildew and Friends Seek Place to Live

- Your refrigerator is a great place for mould, mildew and bacteria to hang out in. Clean it weekly to kill germs that could contaminate food. Use hot, soapy water and lots of elbow grease. Rinse and dry, using clean cloths every time. Evict anything beyond its useful, edible life.

- The sink is home to all sorts of bacteria. Clean the sink drain once or twice a week with a little bleach and water. Pour boiling water down it to melt grease. Think sink. Or you will be sunk.

- The chopping board is a great place for germs to squat. Scrub thoroughly between uses with a brush with hot water and detergent, bung in the dishwasher if it is dishwasher-proof or pour boiling water over it at the end of the day. Deodorize with lemon.

Bay Watch

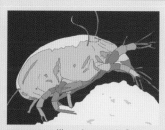

RICE WEEVILS like to hang out in flour, dried pasta, grains, breakfast cereals, rice – i.e. dried pantry staples. Store these in glass, plastic or metal containers with tight-fitting lids to keep them at bay. Talking of bay, some people swear by putting bay leaves in and around the containers of rice, pasta and flour. If you find the food has been badly infested, get rid of it outside. Watch out for flour beetles, too. Slight contaminations are not that harmful but nor are they aesthetically pleasing.

CROAK A ROACH If a cockroach has been in contact with food, discard it. Cockies pick up dangerous micro-organisms as hitchikers. Thumbs down to them. They love living in nooks and crannies, so seal these up. You may need to use a commerical cockroach zapping spray.

Technique Tool Wisdom Cleaning Chore

Shortcuts

 Prepare to Score (on the domestic field)

Maximum score in minimum time. How does that sound? Tempting? 10 out of 10 in 10 minutes takes some beating, guys. Here's a set of Top Trump Tips. Go from hero to zero in no time at all.

10 out of 10 in 10

1 SPILL IT, SWILL IT

If you spill anything on a surface or appliance, give it a wipe with a wet cloth as soon as you can (and that means now!). Next time you use it, you won't have to spend time removing encrusted unpleasantness. It is a bit like wiping your face as soon as you get smudges of food (or lipstick) on it. Make it a reflex. Then you won't get egg on your face...

2 NO TO B.T.H

Boiling the heck out of your food is not a good idea. You waste energy, risk splashing the oven top in non-Jackson Pollock style and over-cooking your food. Cook on a medium heat in a pan that fits the hob or burner. Fewer splashes and spills, more power conserved, easier to clean up afterwards. Great score. You are a Domestic God not an Abstract Artist.

3 MICRO MAGIC

Don't you just hate it when the microwave gets all dirty inside? Use a microwave-safe lid or cling film to prevent Vesuvian-like explosions and put a sheet of kitchen paper inside to catch any escapees. Less mess, less cleaning. More time to open a bottle of bubbly, greet guest(s) and pretend you spent the whole day preparing the meal chained to the stove...

4 DOMESTIC EGGSELLENCE

What is the fastest food in your fridge? No, not the two-minute noodles you are planning to reheat. Don't even go there. Use your noodle – it's an egg. A great thinker once said that eggs is eggs but forgot to say they are full of goodness and boast vitamins A, D and E, protein, calcium, iron, magnesium and phosphorus plus the good fats – poly and mono.

5 DOMESTIC EGGSTACY

Even better news on the 10 over 10 in under 10 front. You can make a romantic weekend breakfast, brunch or TV dinner in 599 seconds. Get the coffee on, mix the Buck's Fizz and boil, poach or scramble a few eggs. Serve with piping hot toast and the newspapers. If you fancy frying instead, use a pan with a heart-shaped mould for the egg.

6 USE YOUR TROLLEY

Next time you are shopping, pop pots of fresh basil and coriander in your trolley. Place on window sill and water according to instructions. Garnish prepared meals with appropriate herb to give that 'just threw together this little dish after work especially for you' look. Tear the leaves by hand rather than chop or cut. It looks more casual and confident.

7 CAPPUCCINO, DARLING?

No need to invest in a budget-breaking space vampire of a coffee machine that makes extra demands on the cleaning front. Just put a small hand-held or a mini-electric whisk (or one of those specially designed move-it-up-and-down froth-making devices) on your Christmas list and your warm milk will look like freshly fallen snow on a crisp wintry day.

8 WOK AROUND THE CLOCK

Cook a delicious and healthy stir-fry in under 10 minutes. Chop garlic, ginger, bean sprouts, spring onions, mangetout peas, carrots, yellow and red peppers (bell peppers) and broccoli and fry in reverse order in a splash of olive oil, moving the contents around the sides of the wok once ready. Splash with soy sauce and serve over noodles. It's chopsticks away, chaps.

9 AVOID SURFACE TENSION

Don't leave food out all day on a worktop to defrost, where it is exposed to germs, airborne insects or Felix the cat. It is safer to remove the food from the freezer the night before and defrost it in the fridge. It takes a minute to do, but if time does not allow you to leave the meat in the fridge for that long, defrost it in the microwave, checking it is thoroughly defrosted.

10 DISH IT UP, DISH IT OUT

Don't use your dishwasher for long-term storage. Never go on vacation with a load of unwashed or even clean equipment in the machine. You never know, the dog or cat might be in there. Empty it as a reflex action and try to store your plates and cutlery close to the machine, so that it is a short walk from one to the other. Makes a huge difference to your motivation.

Do It Together

It is true that a problem shared is a problem halved. It applies within relationships and within the home. Give your relationship 100 per cent. Put in your 50 per cent. It's a simple equation. What other deal would give you that sort of return?

It is reasonable for one partner to expect the other to do their share of the household tasks. Share the chores and share the joys. Partnerships work better when respect and care are involved. Always being the one to load the dishwasher or do the washing up is not going to make you feel respected and cared for. It's another quite simple equation. It may make you feel resentful and upset, taken for granted. That is not good for relationships, romantic or platonic.

We have established that housework keeps you healthy, brings rewards, spices up your love life and makes you more attractive. Divide and drool. Don't just talk about it – it's Chore, Chore not Jaw, Jaw.

Why not draw up a list of the household tasks that need doing and work out who does what, who hates what, who doesn't mind what? Too big an ask? Too much like

Domestic God says ...

If you know your partner really dislikes one particular job, put L or DM. That's compromise. Uh-oh another 'C' word.

hard work? OK, guys, here it is, all done and dusted (well, actually you have to do that bit...)

Photocopy the page and then fill in the boxes as follows – one of you uses the photocopied page (don't argue now!):

L = Like
H = Hate
DM = Don't Mind

Have a look at the completed charts and share the chores so that you have equal amounts of dislikes and likes (no cheating now, guys). Do deals on the Don't Minds. Add any jobs that are missing and apply to your particular circumstances. This exercise is part of the whole process of domestic democracy. Don't start the Chore Wars – be a Domestic Diplomat and do your bit for world peace.

Dirty Devil says ...

If you know your partner really likes one particular job, you may be tempted to put RL against it. That's naughty!

Domestic Democracy

Chore	Like	Hate	Don't Mind
DUSTING			
VACUUMING			
POLISHING			
TIDYING UP			
COOKING			
WASHING UP			
DRYING UP			
LOADING THE DISHWASHER			
EMPTYING THE DISHWASHER			
PUTTING STUFF IN THE CUPBOARDS			
TAKING THE RUBBISH OUT			
SANITIZING THE TRASH BIN			
CLEANING THE SINK			
WASHING THE WALLS			
WASHING WINDOWS			
CLEANING THE SKIRTING BOARDS			
SWEEPING THE FLOOR			
MOPPING THE FLOOR			
CHECKING SUPPLIES			
WRITING THE SHOPPING LIST			
SHOPPING			
PUTTING SHOPPING AWAY			
SHOPPING ON-LINE			
DEFROSTING THE REFRIGERATOR/FREEZER			
CLEANING THE REFRIGERATOR			
CLEANING THE WINDOWS			
CLEANING THE OVEN			
CLEANING THE MICROWAVE			
CHANGING PLUGS			
CARING FOR PLANTS			
RECYCLING			

Wise Dude Mess Mantra

You will know that clutter has reached dangerous levels in the kitchen when you trip up over yesterday's newspaper, an old recipe book, an empty cereal box and that utility bill you keep trying not to pay. It's time to be introduced to a decluttering device, guys. Domestic Dejunk meet Domestic Dude.

Cut the clutter

Everything we bring through into the kitchen needs to be stored somewhere – in the larder, refrigerator, cupboards or trash or perhaps onto the shelves. If you don't do it immediately, clutter will accumulate.

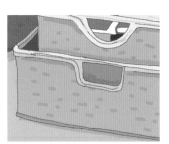

Uncontrolled collecting, unnecessary hoarding and sheer laziness when it comes to containing piles of stuff are all enemies of a tidy kitchen. Excuses about 'no time to tidy up' often occur in kitchens that don't have enough storage space. Newspapers, magazines and books are space vampires in the kitchen. They are visually unattractive (unless you are an abstract artist working in paper), a potential fire hazard and they steal space. So chaps, gather your loincloths, make the decision to clear the clutter, embark upon the mission and divide things into Need and Don't Need piles.

Everthing in the Need pile should be found a home. Divide the Need pile into stuff you use every day and stuff you just can't bear to throw away. Much-used items should be found space in an accessible place, others can be stored in

the loft, under the stairs or elsewhere. The Don't Need pile can go in the trash, but preferably recycle items by distributing them to relatives, friends and charity stores.

Clutter bunnies

Among the worst visible clutter bunnies in the kitchen are old papers, recipe books and magazines, unpaid bills, postcards and letters, little-used equipment, vases of dead or dying flowers, empty packets, half-empty bottles, cans and takeout leftovers and containers without fixed abode or purpose.

Worse still, but largely invisible until the drawers and cupboards in which they are hoarded start to bulge or explode, are the clutter bunnies that lurk and gather, as if conspiring to take over the kitchen. Non-elastic bands, pens and pencils that have retired, non-sticky tape, non-recyclable envelopes, non-reusable corks – you know the sort of thing.

Deal with a drawer or a cupboard per day. Don't tackle the whole lot at once or you will lose courage and motivation. Shifting means removing, not simply re-housing. If you don't need it, dump it. If you do want to keep it, find a proper home for it. File it, label it, store it. Be ruthless, make it roofless. Deal or dump. Love it or leave it. Don't apply this principle to your romantic life.

Temporary storage

Keeping used packaging safely in a designated box for recycling is an effective form of non-permanent storage. If you feel overwhelmed by the idea of de-cluttering your kitchen and putting everything in its final resting place, create some temporary storage and you will feel instantly rewarded.

Organizing the chaos

Once you have sorted your belongings into piles and graded them into levels of need, you can start to store. While temporary storage is good for short-term items, you should decide where permanently required objects need to go.

Need, Don't Need

Use this mantra when you are about to tackle the mess:

DOMESTIC
ENERGY
CAN
LIBERATE
U
TOTALLY.
TIDY
EVERY
ROOM

- Keep a container for instant tidy-ups when your mother visits – log baskets, crates on castors, cardboard storage boxes can all be quickly filled and hidden in the spare room.

- Don't allow any spare surfaces to get piled up with belongings. Do a daily check and scoop up any lost and found items. Contact proper owners.

QED → QAD

QED (*Quod erat demonstrandum*) – people say and read this Latin expression every day (OK, every now and then). 'That which was to be demonstrated' – posh for proof is in the pudding and we've got the pudding, now (for those not in the know yet). Well, in this case, it is QAD (*Question, Answer, Danger*) or watch out 'cos the pudding might be poisoned. The Danger could be a Beware Bacteria, an

Q	A	D
Can I take a steak out of the freezer, defrost it and then put it back in the freezer?	If defrosted thoroughly in the refrigerator, it can be refrozen. Not if defrosted in the microwave or cold water.	The food may have been held at a dangerous temperature if not in the refrigerator. Beware Bacteria!
I'm in the middle of planning a barbie and the raw steak has come into contact with the cold meats and salads.	Keep raw and cooked meat separate. Like supporters of different clubs on a submarine. Deep trouble otherwise.	This sort of cross-contamination can occur easily in the refrigerator or worktop or on the bench itself. Beware Bacteria!
My new partner says my refrigerator stinks and has put a bowl of charcoal inside. Is she dangerous?	There is no problem with charcoal. Compromise with a bowl of freshly-ground coffee on one of the shelves if you are that anxious.	Can't say if she is dangerous per se, but if you keep the door open while deodorizing your fridge with charcoal it won't harm you.
I have just bought a whole chicken to cook for Sunday lunch. Should I wash it before putting in the oven?	No need. What is important is to cook it thoroughly. Make sure juices run clear before serving.	No danger. Any germs will be killed if it is cooked properly.

Amoeba Alert, an early E-Coli warning. It might just be a stink bomb siren. It gets easier once you've read a few, promise. The idea is to alert you to the perils that lurk in the kitchen, perils you may never even have thought of – the domestic dangers waiting to pounce on a daily basis, probably without you even having the slightest notion of their existence. Read before you feed.

Q	A	D
I have defrosted a chicken breast in the refrigerator but now have a hot date. Shall I leave it in the refrigerator or refreeze it?	No, leave it in the fridge and cook it the next day. Don't refreeze. Invite your new friend back for a meal.	Beware Bacteria! You risk getting nasty food poisoning if you refreeze.
My cat's litter tray is in the kitchen. Is this dangerous?	Keep the tray well away from food preparation and consumption zones. Put it in a well-ventilated utility room or in the garage.	Litter trays should not be in kitchens, bedrooms and living areas. They are smelly and full of germs. Wash it outside, frequently.
I have just sliced some raw meat on my chopping board. Can I put the tomatoes on there now to cut up?	No, use a different board or wash it thoroughly after using it to prepare raw chicken or meat.	Beware Bacteria! Germs will be on your hands and on the knife and board. Make sure you wash all three thoroughly.
I am about to go away for the weekend. Can I do the trash when I get back?	No, do it now. Unless you want uninvited housemates to greet you on your return.	Germs love trash (bit like you and the TV). Empty the bin regularly and clean it out with water and disinfectant.

| Technique | Tool | **Wisdom** | Cleaning | Chore |

A Miscellany of Kitchen Wisdom

Wouldn't it be lovely to have a little fountain of wisdom in the kitchen into which you could dip from time to time without getting wet behind the ears? Well, here is the nearest thing to it – a fondue of wisdom, free for all to dip in and out of and back again (if not too cheesy?). Remember, it is not safe to double-dip at real fondue parties but it's OK at metaphorical ones.

Domestic Wisdom from the Man and Woman in the Street

My idea of cleaning the kitchen is to sweep the room with a swift, all-embracing and exhausting glance.
Charles Fipps

A Lieutenant in the Laundry can be a Captain in the Kitchen and a Brigadier in the Bedroom. He will still await promotion in the Bathroom.
A Ellis

The last thing a smart man needs in the kitchen-diner is a dumb waiter.
Annabel Pilkington

No man ever came to enormous harm from his partner while washing or drying the dishes.
Alice B Foster

A piece of paper on the worktop can be informative and healthy. But who wants piles in the kitchen?
Mal Peachey

If a man's home is his castle, his bathroom may be the moat and his cellar the dungeon, but his bedroom does not have to be the torture chamber and his kitchen the pigsty.
Arthur Holmes

Food Wise, Food Safe, Food Fun

Treat your dinner party like a rock concert. Serve a light starter as a support band to tickle people's fancy and whet their appetite for the big gig. Follow with an exciting, fulfilling headliner of a main dish, and then savour the dessert encore. Listen for cries of 'More...' Get the roadies to do the washing up.

Think of your menu as a painter's palette, a sort of edible still life by, say, Joan Miró or Pablo Picasso. Think tomatoes and basil, green salad garnished with oranges, meat and two highly-coloured veg. It's oral eye candy. Tomato soup, followed by pasta napolitana and a red pepper salad, strawberries in a red-berry coulis, washed down with Campari, red wine and port is just too red.

If a dinner party goes badly, refrigerate leftovers and eat the next day. Don't risk food poisoning by leaving them out of the refrigerator overnight.

Check if guests are vegetarian, vegan, allergic to certain foods. It saves awkward, embarrassed or downright panic-stricken moments at the table. If you know any seedarians, invite them for drinks only.

Folding an omelette is like folding a piece of A4 paper. Ensure the omelette does not stick to the pan by using a good non-stick one or a generous amount of butter or margarine to cook it with. Take a delicate spatula (avoiding metal implements that may damage the surface of the pan and the mood of your partner) to fold 33.33% (recurring) a.k.a a third towards the centre of the delicous, just-the-right-shade-of-yellow omelette. Repeat on the other side. Serve and savour.

Wisdometer

CHECK BATTERY-OPERATED SMOKE ALARMS weekly and electric ones every month. Replace batteries twice a year. Put it on the chore chart. Keep the grille of the smoke detector clean, too.

Always check the manufacturer's instructions on equipment. The booklets are included for a purpose. Nota Bene, mate, or buy a Latin Dictionary. Check how to use a fire extinguisher and where plus how to install, test, use and maintain.

Always check safety instructions for electrical equipment and keep all the literature in one safe place – leaflets, guarantees and emergency phone numbers.

Check regularly for bare wires on appliances and get them sorted. Always check that plugs and leads are not near heat, flame or water.

Index

Alcohol	21, 47	kitchen	12	storing	27
Annual chores	18	microwave oven	54	utensils	28-33
Ants	53	oven	12	Eyes	20
Arms	21	refrigerator	38		
		stain-removal	60-61	Floor cloths	25, 53
Bacteria	53, 66-67	walls	58-59	Floors:	
Beeton, Mrs Isabella	7	windows	12, 57	stain-removal	60
Bilberries	20	Cloths	13, 25, 27, 53	washing	56-57
Bins	24, 26	Clutter	72-73	Food	21
Body	21	Cockroaches	24, 67	defrosting	40-41
Brownie points	14	Cocktails	50-51	preparation	47
Buck's Fizz	51	Coffee	40, 69	Food pyramid	46-47
Bugs	66-67	Cork floors	56-57	Freezer	40-41
Burning calories	15, 21			Frozen food	40-41
Burns	21	Daily chores	19	Fruit	47
		Dangers	74-75		
Calories	15, 21	Declutter	72-73	Garlic	20
Canned foods	44-45	De-junking	9	Germs	55, 66-67
Carpets	56	Diet	46-47	Glasses	34-35
Carrots	20	Dinner party	77	Grater	28
Carving	48-49	Dirty cloths	25		
Casserole dish	33	Dirty dishes	9, 24, 52-53	Hands	21
Cavemen	9, 10	Dishcloths	13, 25, 27, 53	Hardwood floors	57
Ceilings, cleaning	58-59	Dishwasher	69	Herbs	12, 63, 69
Chicken, carving	48-49	Drinks	21, 47	frozen	41
Chopping board	67	Dusting	8	Houseplants	62-63
Chores:				Hygiene:	
chart	18-19, 71	Eggs	39, 68, 69	kitchen	12, 24-27
sharing	70-71	Electrical appliances	77	personal	20-21
Cleaning:		Equipment:		for pet owners	66
ceilings	58-59	knives	30-31		
floors	56-57	pans	32-33	Kitchen	12-13
				bugs	66-67

hygiene	12, 24-27
no-nos	24-25
storage	27
Kitchen equipment	28-33
Kitchen routine	22-23
Kitchen sink	8, 67
Knives	30-31
Larder	44-45
Laundry basket	8
Learning	14
Leftovers:	
chicken and turkey	49
wine	41
Linoleum floors	57
Long-term tasks	9
Microwave ovens	68
cleaning	54
Mildew	67
Miscellany of wisdom	76-77
Mission statement	9
Monthly chores	18
Mould	67
Mouth	21
Nose	20
Onions	21
Oven mitts	21
Ovens	12, 54
Paintwork,	
stain-removal	61
Pans	32-33
size	26

washing	53
Paper towels	53
Pasta measurer	29
Pasta server	29
Pepper mill	28
Pestle and mortar	29
Pests	53
Pets	64-65
Pizza cutter	28
Plants	12, 62-63
Questionnaire	16-17
answers	80
Refreezing	40
Refrigerator thermometer	39
Refrigerators	13, 67
cleaning	38
contents	42-43
history	36-37
modern facilities	38
using	39
Reheating takeout	55
Rewards	11
Rice weevils	67
Roasting tin	33
Romance	9
Routine	22-23
Rugs	57
Shortcuts	68-69
Sink	8, 67
Smoke alarms	77
Spices	21
Spills	68
Stain removal	60-61
Stir-fries	69

Storage	27, 73
Store-cupboard	44-45
Takeout, reheating	55
Tea towels	13, 25, 53
Thermometer, fridge	39
Tools:	
knives	30-31
pans	32-33
utensils	28-29
Top-to-toe hygiene	20-21
Towels	25
Trash	24, 26
Utensils	28-29
Vacuuming	56
Vegetables	47
Walls:	
cleaning	58-59
stain-removal	61
Washing up	9, 24, 52-53
Water	47
Weekly chores	19
Weevils	67
Windows, cleaning	12, 57
Wine, leftovers	41
Wine glasses	34-35
Wok	33
Work surfaces	25, 27

Do you know it all already?

QUIZ ANSWERS

HOW LONG SHOULD YOU GENERALLY LEAVE AN OPENED JAR OF FOOD IN THE
REFRIGERATOR?
A

WHY SHOULD YOU REMOVE DUST REGULARLY FROM SURFACES?
C

WHEN DID YOU LAST EMPTY THE TRASH?
A

IS YOUR DOG MORE HYGIENIC THAN YOU?
B (OR E)

WHEN SHOULD YOU DO THE WASHING UP?
A

WHY SHOULD YOU VENTILATE YOUR KITCHEN REGULARLY?
E

WHY DO YOU NEED TO INSTALL A SMOKE DETECTOR?
B

WHEN DID YOU LAST CLEAN YOUR REFRIGERATOR?
D

SCIENTISTS HAVE FOUND THAT THE MALE BRAIN DOESN'T REGISTER DUST. IS THIS BECAUSE:
A (OR E OR D)

WHAT IS YOUR MESS MOTTO?
A